M

Why
Breathe?

Clem J. Nagel & Elizabeth C. Nagel

Why Breathe?

©2011 Clem J. Nagel • Elizabeth C. Nagel
First Edition October 2011
ISBN 978-0-9835370-1-4

Photography: North Shore Lake Superior
Elizabeth C. Nagel

Brief portions of this book
may be reproduced
for one time use only.
Otherwise no portion may be used
without the writers' permission.

Also by
Clem J. Nagel

*Listen for the Silence:
A Walk Through the Natural World*

Prairie Sky Prairie Ground

Previously published:
Custody of the Eyes, Minneapolis Star Tribune;
Grampa's Flower, Labyrinth Pathways;
Great Horned Owl Vigil, Black Gold, Kingfisher

Also by
Elizabeth C. Nagel

*There is No Future in the Past:
A Travel Memoir*

Waiting for the Heat to Pass

*The Labyrinth and the Enneagram:
Circling into Prayer
(with Jill K.H. Geoffrion)*

Book design: Judith Connor Design
connordesign@visi.com

For our grandchildren
Ben, Sam, and Grace
Henry and Geo

You inherit from our generation
a world swirling with accelerating change.
Never stop asking questions.

Contents

CHAPTER THREE
~ Looking Deeper ~
Elizabeth Nagel

•

CHAPTER FOUR
~ Voices of Prophetic Poetry ~
Clem Nagel

•

~ *Interlude* ~
Clem Nagel & Elizabeth Nagel

CHAPTER EIGHT
~ Soul Under Construction ~
Clem Nagel

•

CHAPTER NINE
~ Cycles of Life ~
Elizabeth Nagel

•

INTRODUCTION

After the Second World War, the war that was supposed to be the last war, our respective families moved to the same small prairie town in western Minnesota. We grew up together, fell in love, and married. Being poets or writers was not something we ever imagined. We had other plans for our lives.

But poetry found us, as the poet Pablo Neruda said about himself. Our first poems were personal, just for us. Then Clem began to give away his poetry and Elizabeth discovered that others found her poetry spoke to them. We both continued writing — and began publishing our work. Several books followed from each of us.

Along the way, we discovered the joy (and the challenge) of being writing colleagues, critiquing and editing each other's work. This book is a natural outgrowth of our shared lives as poets. What better way to express ourselves but in its collaboration.

The title is both a question *(Why Breathe?)* and an exclamation *(Why Breathe!)*. The first expression is the rhetorical and non-answerable question. What calls each of us to arise in the morning to go about our ordinary lives? The world is chaotic, often painful, and sometimes a source of despair. How do we respond to what we encounter — how do we continue to come back to taking a deep breath and going on?

The second expression is our answer to the question. Throw yourselves upon life. Celebrate its surprises and its possibilities. In the midst of the accelerating rate of change in the world as we know it, flowing with what opens up before us, means breathing deep, paying attention, looking inward, and then being willing to contribute our voices to the world's needs.

It is this world that we have to give to our grandchildren. Our generation has made mistakes that have taught us wisdom and made positive contributions far too long to enumerate. At the same time all of us have lived quite ordinary lives. For us, our respective lives bring us back to the question *Why Breathe?* held within this greater context of celebrating life.

— Clem Nagel/Elizabeth Nagel

CHAPTER ONE

~ Travels of the Heart ~
Elizabeth Nagel

Journeys on the road
bring unexpected rewards
for those who listen

~

Challenges aren't free
the cost may be very high
pack light, expect much

~

Open windows wide
dress warm, laugh loudly, eat well
wind blows through the heart

Road Trip

Sometimes the urge takes over
to hit the road, move beyond
my comfort zone — and remember

mountains, massive beyond memory
blotchy with last winter's snow and recent
white sprinklings of weather passing through.

Mountain roads winding through canyons
and over passes, distance measured in time
not straight lines between two points, where

red rock is carved by wind and rain
into fantastic shapes, obliterating radio signals
and connections with the familiar.

Vistas that can be recorded only in the mind
canyons no match for hundreds of miles
of landscape stretched out in clear, arid air.

People whose daily lives bear little resemblance
to mine, foreign as if from far distant lands
yet cast from the same human mold

whose voices in small cafes carry accents that are
immediate indicators of their origins in
a homogenized world of blue jeans, and t-shirts

cell phones tucked in back pockets
cowboy hats, donned first thing in the morning
or caps advertising essential ranch products.

The road home is always different
because I have changed through my experiences and
encounters on the road, shaken loose from the familiar.

— Elizabeth

Santa Fe

the plaza is ready
for annual summer festivals,
newly-sodded thick green grass
covers the ground, keep-off-grass signs
ignored by everyone seeking shade,
a gathering place for strolling teens
with cell phones and skateboards,
musicians, tourists, and food vendors
find their places among benches
that invite people-watching,
ice cream savored in arid heat,
native peoples' hand-crafted jewelry
spread on blankets at the Governor's Palace,
galleries radiate from the plaza
filled with work generated by
the particular blend of artistic energy
pervading this northern New Mexican place

every time,
I return asking the same question:
what created this space like no other,
fostering such extraordinary creativity?

— Elizabeth

patience

the mountain waits
as it has waited since
earth-forces pushed it
upward into the clouds

it neither asks nor takes —

waiting until the crushing weight
of ice creates glaciers which
require cycles of snow
to carve its face

the silent witness of
the waiting mountain
produces beauty beyond
human imagination
patience its proclamation

the mountain teaches me to wait
cast away my illusions of
being in control of forces
at work beyond me
those that carve my face

neither do I beg nor plead
for exemption from what is
nor grasp in greed
my imagined version
of who I think I am

— Elizabeth

holy Ganges

from small beginnings
high in the Himalayas
the holy Ganges flows downward,
gathering sacred energy and pilgrims
along its way to the sea

tonight in my imagination
it draws me to its banks,
one more pilgrim seeking
healing from its waters,
even though I sit half a world away,
white snow drifting past my window

in my mind's eye, I imagine
fashioning small paper boats,
one for each event and person
from a dark spiral of my life, years
when I lost my way among people
intent on furthering themselves,
twisting truth into half-truths
until I could believe nothing

in each paper boat I place
a white votive candle and light it,
gently I place my small vessels
one by one in its opaque waters
saturated with the body-energy of
centuries of pilgrims, trailing
my fingers behind each boat as
they flow downriver

I watch in silence, each delicate
creation carries away
my letting go of what was.
sitting on into the evening as
images of the last small candlelight
vanish in the soft dusk,
sacred water takes away
a past done and finished

holy Ganges, you flow within me
with all these countless pilgrims
who surround me, each seeks,
each finds within them
what they do not expect

— Elizabeth

Cape Hatteras Gale

after the November storm
dredged up long-lost debris,
we walked the barrier islands
prying loose from the sand
a tree-snag impregnated with
sea salt and water, taking both
of us to drag it above
the high tide mark

we brushed sand from its crevices
to carry it on other journeys
as we moved from place to place
a reminder of the power of
sea-wind and sand between our toes
and places long ago when we emerged
from the sea, its water coursing
through our veins

— Elizabeth

8

CHAPTER TWO

~ Voices from Nature ~
Clem Nagel

Before spring sunrise
a robin was caroling
music of the soul

~

Gulls snatch small mole crabs
from returning ocean waves
quick lunch on the run

~

Nesting lone snowflake
waiting among green pine boughs
others soon arrive

Hiking a Rim of Canyon de Chelly

The towering pinnacle of Spider Rock
rises from canyon floor and
glows deep red in the sun.

The scents of pinion pine and juniper
mingle with the smell
of my perspiration.

My hands caress smooth
gray skins of ancient
twisted, tree trunks.

The taste of remnants of
morning's trail breakfast
stuck between my teeth.

The silent sound of air through wings
of ravens skimming past
nearby cliff alcoves.

I imagine the quiet
that wisps of clouds might make —
if I were close enough.

— Clem

Springtime Chorale

Soft green buds cover
leafless trees.
Silent pussy willows bloom,
quiet catkins haloed by sun.

The incessant, unseen chorus —
begins its concert.

An unfrozen wood frog reflects
its formal name, *Rana sylvatica*,
leaves its woodland winter den
to search for
thawed March water.
Hosts of other frogs join in.

As I watch,
one lone frog hops from leaf-covered
woods,
crosses a sand road to add its presence
to the eons-old spring procession.

Water shimmers. Their submerged,
moving bodies, hidden from view,
are belied only by ripples.

Their underwater advances create
pulses of private waves.
One frog leaps ahead,
then another . . . and another . . . and another
only to submerge once again

among brown grasses,
last year's cattails, and
underwater stems
soon to be coated with
egg clusters.

Singing fills the air.
Their chortling invites me to
join their laughter —
to lighten up a little
after a long, hard winter.

— Clem

ascent

butterflies seem
more beautiful this August
maybe their emergence from
a summer of great overcast
smoggy skies
ominous clouds

after mind-clearing rains
the skies have cleared
butterflies dart, flutter, glide
to shine in the sun

a single swallowtail lingers
on a patch of phlox
by the pond, searching out
newly emerged
pink resurrection lilies

I watch the animated
patch of yellow
circle the flower garden
before its vertical ascent
to greet the
still blue sky.

— Clem

Great Horned Owl Vigil

Under a cold
February moon,
a secluded forest tree
anchors the owls'
borrowed, flimsy nest.

Silent after courtship,
their night-time shapes
ferociously guard
a precious future.
Under soft feathers,
two or three round,
dusty-white eggs
hatch.

Now —
they watch for intruders
and promises of
meager food.

— Clem

last snow of the season

a lone daffodil bud
pierces brown leaf litter

unfolds toward
sun and warmth

then knighted
with a crown of snow

it bends low with grace
for the moment —

I am so honored
this early spring morning

to be greeted
by one lone daffodil

I return its bow
before it sheds its snow

— Clem

— Written on Earth Day, 2011

Cerulean

A small flutter of a bird
    traverses a tree top.

Part of a springtime passing-through
    to elsewhere.

My eyes lift skyward to glimpse
    its ethereal, sky-blue back.

But, I see only
    a clear, white breast.

The warbler
    moves northward.

Next year, I will walk
    along a high-ridge trail,

overlooking tree tops.

                        — Clem

Natural Dietary Supplements

I see the roadside gumweed is
already in full bloom —
a month ahead of usual.

Its golden, sunny flowers attract
many insects that become
entrapped in its odorous, sticky,
enzyme-laden, involucral bracts.

Some surmise that
gumweed is quite unique
to supplement its
usual diet of sun, water,
soil, and air —
with bug juice.

— Clem

Black Gold

Late winter
late in day
when spring seems remote.

Cold lone tree
washed in golden-
rayed sunset.
Silent crow-silhouettes
cover tips of branches —
like buds.

— Clem

Almost In Utah

I pause to listen to
whispers of butterfly wings
among unfamiliar flowers

and watch a brown lizard
poise motionless on
a sun-bathed, red rock.

I wonder who placed a
rock cairn at the entrance of
the small dirt road I
chose to take?

A distant raven calls —
I depart in silence,
leaving the small lizard
undisturbed.

— Clem

Windswept

Windswept barrier islands,
   lie below a cold, diffuse, gray sky.
The rush of beige-jade waves,
   sequentially crest, pause and curl —
   just before their downward plunge.
Water churned into
   murky turbulence.

Sandwiched between
   sky and sea,
   pelicans, with wings set,
   deftly skim the wind,
   following wave troughs.

Wind-whipped froth
   skitters along wet sand
   as if with a mind of its own.
The iridescent bubbles linger —
   just a moment.

Sandpipers run, stop and
   balance on the feet of their
   water-mirrored selves.
Then hurrying seaward,
   discover food between
   fresh new waves' return.

With sand-laden waves kicked up
  higher than the horizon,
  the earth strives
  to become airborne.

Greeting the air like a
  leaping gazelle.

— Clem

— *Elizabeth and I were at the end of the beach road on South Padre Island one mid-February. The weather was very cold for the islands' permanent residents (coldest on record!), windy, and foggy.*

CHAPTER THREE

~ Looking Deeper ~
Elizabeth Nagel

Quiet fog draws close
drives expansive travel dream
into inner space

~

I stand in the middle of the meadow covered
with the summer flowers of the short mountain
season. My eyes blur with tears, remembering all
the times I have been in this place.

seeing outside blurs
the heart invites eyes inward
then insight arrives

~

Seas of fall grasses
ripple across open fields
soft winds caress cheeks

not mine to take

my hand plunges into rushing water
grows numb, with snow-melt
rushing to somewhere it has never been

I wrench loose the beautiful rock
its colors and patterns entrance
as I turn it over in my hand
washing away mud and gravel
from where it adhered to the stream bottom

after its journey in my right pocket
dried by the fabric of my pants
I place my treasure with reverence
on a shelf where I stare at it, its brilliance
diminished without its water film

I wonder what I saw on its surface —
and wish I'd left it where it belongs

— Elizabeth

Dreamcatchers

Remote peaks of southern Chile, draped
with perpetual snow, snow compressed
into glacial ice, relentless winds bearing
cold Pacific moisture high into
hidden crevasses to replenish summer snows.

Unnamed masses of volcanic rock stretch
far into clouds, only soaring condors
keep watch. What dreams do
these massive mountains harbor, waiting
in silence for winter's bitter cold?

> *Do these mystical mountains*
> *catch night-dreams, blown across*
> *continents and the waters connecting them?*
> *Dreams stripped of endless words, carried*
> *by wind that drives the sea northward*
> *along Chile's remote, uninhabited coast.*

> *Do these mountains of incredible beauty*
> *capture our prayers of hope and peace*
> *and hurl them through the clouds?*
> *Into the energy of the universe*
> *to be caught by ancient stars and*
> *sent back in altered forms.*

— Elizabeth

held in the fog

Fog hangs over the lake
so still, nothing moves.
I crawl from the tent, stretch,
stand on a boulder
not wanting my presence
to create a ripple

The fog is my teacher, its fingers
drift across meadows and still waters
willing me to be in the now,
no plans, no agenda, temporary —
teaching me where my wisdom lies

I carry this fog-bound space
with me, over years in which
sometimes I lack wisdom to know
when to speak out or when to remain silent —
years of stretching for voice

— Elizabeth

Silence's Challenge

Sounds first grow louder
when I sit to meditate,
then slip away under my awareness.

I talk back to the silence,
tell it to go away because it is
dangerous. Torn between
listening and not listening.
Fears of what I may hear,
as the deafening silence crawls out
from under a chair to sit at my feet.

Too old to waste time
avoiding my fears,
the clock's pulse reminds me
that time does not function
as calculus, moving toward infinity
but never arriving.
One day my life will end
   or what I know life to be.

So I say to the visage
that sits at my feet —
         hello friend.

— Elizabeth

The Book Signing

She lingers just beyond
the table where I was signing books
until everyone moved on.
She is a slight woman, dressed
in worn clothes, faded as her hair.
She asks what I am doing,
her smile shy, a few teeth missing.
> *I wrote a poem once.*
> *After my mother died.*

I reply that her mother
must have been very special to her.
> *Oh, yes! It was hard,*
> *writing that poem.*
> *Hard to make the lines rhyme.*

I ask about her mother.
Her words pour out.
> *She had chickens*
> *and would go out back,*
> *catch one and wring its neck.*

With her hands, she demonstrates
how her mother wrung chicken necks.

I ask if she ever tried
writing another poem and
if she knew the words
did not have to rhyme.
When I show her
one of my poems
she just smiles her shy smile.

Perhaps one poem in a lifetime
is enough, enough when it is
about your mother
whom you miss so much.

— Elizabeth

Secret Fantasy

The orchestra assembles.

Musicians find their seats,
check instruments, reeds, music.
The audience rustles with anticipation.
At the periphery, the tympani stand ready.
Their copper sides gleam under the lights,
full of promise and taut as
a woman's belly nine months pregnant.
Their player bends an ear to the heads,
listens, adjusts, tunes.
The concertmaster rises and the oboe plays an A,
a hush falls over the hall.
The conductor strides across the stage,
bows, and picks up the baton.

let the music begin!

I always have yearned to play the tympani.
I would stand behind them at attention,
feet planted firmly, arms folded
across my chest, mallets held upright
in my right hand, one eye on the music
the other on the conductor, poised for my cue.
Bending over slightly, I would produce
a soft roll like the whisper of distant thunder,
or raise my mallets high and
come crashing down in a roaring fortissimo
full of color and excitement!

I would play all the great concert halls
round the world from the gleaming
Avery Fisher Hall at Lincoln Center and
Vienna's stately Koncerthaus and
its resplendent Musikverein,
to the rotund Royal Albert in London, and
Hungary's Esterhazy with its rococo elegance.
The sounds of my tympani would reverberate
through historic Boston Symphony Hall,
and the amazing acoustics of
Amsterdam's Concertgebouw.
I would perform everything from Mozart to Mahler,
especially Beethoven's 5th and Bartok's 4th.

Sometimes when the audience stands and
shouts Bravo, the conductor will point
his baton at me and I will discretely bow.
Critics, giving my orchestra a heads up,
will mention the superb contributions
my tympani gave to the performance.

Sighing, I settle back in my red plush seat
at Orchestra Hall, program notes clutched
in my hands, waiting for the performance to begin.
Thankful my secret fantasy
is someone else's dream come true.

let the music begin!

— Elizabeth

what does it mean to die?

I look around and know

to die is never again
look into faces of those I love,
never again smell spring upon the air,
know the warmth of another's touch,
or my lover's caress, never
again search daily for
annual resurrections of spring bulbs
or smell lilacs outside my bedroom window,
their winter buds fat with anticipation,
or gaze amazed at a sunset sky

to die is never again love another
or enjoy laughter of friends around
the intimacy of a shared meal
of good food, listen to heart stirrings
mine or someone else's,
never again enjoy
the exhilaration of life's challenges,
the deep satisfaction of growth
nor feel tears flowing down my cheeks

to die is to never carry the wind in my hair
while I walk edges of the sea,
or see the sun reflecting off
the colors of a red-tailed hawk,
nor hear again the music
I carry in my soul

to die is to
forever relinquish
these small joys

for these losses, I weep

— Elizabeth

are we only stories?

our stories run through each other,
changing, as they touch other stories
shorter, longer, reframed,
disguised truths
added and discarded
raising questions,
they challenge other stories

are we only stories?
pieces of maps, whose
destinations are long forgotten,
or are our stories fragments
of our essence
offered up on life's altars?

— Elizabeth

unused words

strange sea creatures
live in pure darkness below

unidentifiable birds hide
within vague field marks

stones lie long-buried
under debris of rock slides

my camera lens captures images
while I focus elsewhere

stories remain hidden
in my mind's recesses

until they slip out on pages
words I did not know I had

— Elizabeth

Living in Gratitude

My life overflows with goodness,
as a quilt gathered around me as I sit before a winter fire.
The love of my beloved, times spent together
on the road, collecting glimpses of small jewels
flitting among trees and subtle browns of hawks
soaring overhead, heralding spring migrations.
So much goodness. I offer up my gratitude.

I live immersed in a tapestry of senses,
the intoxication of high desert colors, walking
barefoot for hours along the sea's edge,
the sensuous feel of saltwater upon my skin.
I inhale mountain fragrance and piney north woods,
marvel at small quiet wonders breaking through
black earth to salute tender spring-green leaves above
that came to clothe the sculpture of winter trees.
I plant, wait for my vegetables to display their glory,
before the deep colors of fall call forth
the season's first silent snowfalls.
How can life be so good?

There are books, books, books, more books
that captivate my mind and call me to writing,
absorbed in the play with words, until I must clear out
meditative space and just be. The pleasure of being able
to walk again, never taking for granted what once I never
noticed. Good food and conversations, sounds
of laughter gathering up friends and family,
before I curl up at night in my beloved's arms.
Such gratitude. My life overflows.

— Elizabeth

CHAPTER FOUR

~ Voices of Prophetic Poetry ~
Clem Nagel

Egrets watch backhoes
dig foundation holes in marsh
silent witnesses

~

Distant airplane sounds
remind me of disasters.
Apprehension flies
in face of serenity.
Breathe in, breathe out, notice peace.

~

The heart speaks wisdom
world peace grows from compassion
not from war's absence

Watchful Attentiveness

Be then, ever watchful for
what has never
happened before.

Take second glances —
and third.
Truly perceive and appreciate
with compassion.

See the emergence of
evolving life forms.

Be the first
to sense a lightening of spirit
after the hoping-against-hope of
those depressed,
groaning under the weight
of illness, oppression,
and war.

Follow rivers as they
almost imperceptibly
course new pathways,
struggling to regenerate
to preserve their integrity.

Watch glacial boulders
being cracked by frozen water,
eroded by lichens,
weathered,
ground to dust.

Pay attention to baby-blue ice
revealed to warming light
as glaciers calve and
melt water gushes from ice caves
and flowers rush to grow on
new-found ground.

Have eyes open wide to
receive first photons of
fresh light
from far-flung stars.

Glimpse a baby's
first fleeting smile
after leaving
the womb.

Watch for the time
when all death row
countdowns are banned
by reason of human decency —
if for nothing else.

Imagine the moment when
peace finally embraces
generations that have long lived
knowing only terror and hunger
and disease and bombs and
desolation and
death.

Hold all these.
Hold all these
new incipient things
in your heart.

Hold them close.
Imagine them, name them whatever you will —
as a way to
slip into
the sacred.
And
through it all

May peace and peace and peace be everywhere.
(The Upanishads 600 BC)

— Clem

—Written on the birthday of Martin Luther King Jr.,
1/15/2006

Sometimes We Dream

What would it take
everyday for the sky to
bloom hydrangea-blue?

What would be necessary
for a boat to sail
round the world in
waters of peace?

What would happen
if a fairy fell asleep,
would its wings
crumple and tear?

Sometimes —
we must live outside
the frame of what is known
and into our dreams.

— Clem

Custody of the Eyes

They walk.
They walk back and forth.
Back and forth in the hot sun
near the shadows of
downtown churches.
It is a measured walk
along well-worn dirt paths,
next to turn lanes,
off busy highways.

Parallel lives to mine.
Except —
they stow their belongings
behind them, held safe by
chain-link fences.

Someone's children.
Asking for handouts.
Holding tattered signs —
God Bless.
Need money for medicine.
Homeless vet.
God Bless.

They come toward me
from parallel universes —
eyes unblinking,
intent on contact with mine.

Their faces look so familiar.
Best to keep my eyes
to myself, lest
my heart respond.

They know
I see them —
as do I.

Their faces
so familiar —
so familiar.

God Bless.

— Clem

— *Written on the United Nation's World Day of Peace , 2006*

What Goes Around

I

Tires wear thin,
spinning off rubber dust.
Particulate matter
released
to join soil, water,
air, and
lungs.

Disaster unseen —
insidious, interstitial,
pollution.

II

The heavy vise-like tool,
slips from an astronaut's grip.
Released to orbit.
Assumed
never-to-be-seen-again.
After three days —
a fifteen-pound emergency
looms.

Shuttle rockets fire to avoid
an insipient disaster
almost not seen.

III

Hazy, dull, yellow-orange sphere
hangs in the sky.
North African desert storm
lofted high the 2.5 micrometer-wide
dust motes.
Traversed the ocean
to block the sun's rays
over five Midwestern states.

Last night's sunset —
the most glorious ever seen.

IV

What goes around,
comes around.

— Clem

Tethered to the Future?

The tourist bus makes a scheduled
stop at a small roadside restaurant
with snow-capped peaks in the
distance. We have an hour to explore.

One lone sheep is free
to move about
near the restaurant, a barbecue
firepit on display to those inside.

Free to graze on self-cropped grass,
the sheep is tethered to a short chain
that
slides along
a long cable running between
a shed and an iron stake anchored
near the glass-walled smokehouse.

Through the barbecue pit windows
I see a splayed carcass
a lamb wired to
a metal cross —
suspended above a pungent,
smoldering heap of ashes.
Outside, neatly stacked piles
of chopped wood are ready to
keep the fire alive.

The lone sheep walks toward
the smokehouse window
framing the butchered lamb.
It pauses, then turns to
look back at me, bleating
his greeting — pleading.

The moment gives me pause . . .
In what tethered state
might we all be?

I divert my eyes to
snow-capped peaks and
look at my watch.

After an hour,
not too soon,
we move on —
knowing the next day
we would cruise
to outlying islands,

weather permitting . . .

— Clem

— Written after a restaurant stop along the southern-most section
   of the Pan-American Highway, just north of Ushuaia, Argentina,
   above South America's Cape Horn.

dis asters

sometimes I wonder why I keep things

things of which I know little
or fear to know more

like a small crumble of red brick
I took from a pile of rubble

I know I should have
left it where it lay

but it already was broken
and there were so many

just as lives once filled
long rows of barracks

the museum with pictures
and all the shoes

and signs in languages
I didn't know

why I chose that broken brick
near children's Block #66

I do not know

not often, I still hold that red remnant
and wonder why I keep it

why do I keep memories of my escape
from those memorial grounds

when I ate a sandwich seated
on a gray boulder on a sunny hillside

overlooking a far-distant river
watching a storm pass through the valley

why did I feel unsafe, when I became aware
my discarded granite boulder

was one of ten jumbled stone block letters
that once spelled Buchenwald

behind me more letters, over my shoulder
I felt the empty guardhouse watchtower

why do I remember myriads of blue asters
peering past tangles of rusty barbed-wire

feeling safe outside the compound's fence
knowing I could go home and would

sometimes I wonder why I keep things
that never should have been

I do not know

*The best remedy for those who are afraid, lonely,
or unhappy is to go outside, somewhere where they
can be quiet, alone with the heavens, nature and God.
Because only then
does one feel that all is as it should be.*
— Anne Frank 1929-1945

— Clem

An Incredible Sadness

On Sunday morning.
Red, white, and blue lights
flash just behind
an old, white car
pulled over on the shoulder
of the northbound interstate.

My eyes catch a glimpse of
a highway trooper
approaching a sobbing,
brown-skinned woman
sitting alone in the car —
face hidden in her hands.

Why do I feel so sad
this glorious, sun-filled day
when I pass them by?

Does she lack money
to pay a fine?
Has she no license to drive?

Or, is she
an illegal human being —
on her way to
nowhere?

Red, white, and blue.

— Clem

54

The-Well-Meaning-Ones: A Rant

Why do some *well-meaning-ones*
    do things they don't believe,
    get carried away with
    feathering their own nests,
    faithfully feeding the strong
    and allow weak ones to
        languish and wither?

Why do some of those
    well-meaning-ones we know well
    refuse to speak up or
    scream out to be heard,
    refuse to give voice to those who
        are afraid to speak?

Why do some of us *well-meaning-ones*
    conveniently look the other way,
    pretend we don't hear,
    turn a blind eye to injustice?

Why do *well-meaning-ones*
    those-of-us-with-voice,
    choose to whisper,
        all alone in
            box canyons?

                      — Clem

INTERLUDE

Sandhill cranes, standing three to four feet tall, are one of the oldest bird species in the world. We have sought these cranes out in their wintering grounds, from Aransas National Wildlife Refuge on the Texas Gulf Coast to Bosque del Apache Wildlife Refuge in central New Mexico. During their spring migration, we have gone to central Nebraska and joined other people who come from around the world to observe their majesty. There along a sixty mile stretch of the Platte River, a half million cranes gather to fatten up before heading northward to the Arctic, where they spread out to breed from Siberia to all across northern Canada.

When we began to compile poems for this book, it was not surprising to discover we had both written about these fascinating birds. Rather than choose one poem over the other, we decided to merge our images and memories. We wove our two poems together, a few lines at a time, to produce a seamless whole. Not quite the same as writing a poem together, something we have never tried!

The result is a poetic tribute to these birds who pair for life - and who keep track of their mate by beginning and answering each other in immense flocks of thousands of birds, which the cranes form during spring migration.

Springtime Ritual

For eons, sandhill cranes have gathered
in the springtime safety of
the Platte River's braided shallows.
Here along the ancient river
old snow sinks into the ground.
No longer needed is the warmth
of wintering marshes.

At sunrise these ancient cranes
fly out to farm land, where
they gorge themselves with last year's corn
and insects, frogs, snails, and unwary rodents
before their long journey northward
to breeding grounds.
Territories staked out when they first mated.

When the sun falls toward the horizon,
the cranes fly from nearby fields.
Threads of gray stream through
the evening sky and descend
to the Platte's sunset- burnished waters.

They take their places
in a cacophony of raucous greetings.
Their conversations fill the universe
until the sound defeats any chance of
spoken words, their exchanges
resonating in observers' bones.

The cranes join their reflections
in shallow waters, and execute
a ballet of dances, tossing limp weed strands
at their life-mates —
hints of their soon northward journey.

Throughout the night, they stand in the river,
crane-fashion on one leg.
Sentinels placed at intervals among them
listen for the splash of predators,
taking turns as if by some prearranged roster.
While they dream of severe northern places,
of building nests of mounded vegetation
spaced out across the Arctic tundra .

For now, the cranes wait.
Lives secure over eons.
Now in present time
they rehearse for the future.

On the tundra, they will dance
their millennial courtship,
wooing each other as if each spring were the first.
Jumps into the air, bows to their partners,
they prance and spread their large wings.
Graceful plumes and red caps they wear,
speak of a loyalty to
their chosen one.

Something within us
insists on opening wings —
soaring far beyond.

— Clem and Elizabeth

CHAPTER FIVE

~ Eyes Wide Open ~
Elizabeth Nagel

Paying attention
awakens all the senses
surprises abound

~

Rivers overflow
brown rushing water surges
covering the land
stealing the homes of many
reality swept away

~

The invitation
includes all of creation
only some respond

unlikely gifts

etched on my interior landscape
are all those places
my feet have touched
as I wandered the globe,
places where I have dug with my hands
into rich, dark soil to plant the future,
fat daffodil bulbs deer refuse to eat,
spring vegetables and all their fall bounty,
childhood attempts
to dig straight to China

indelible places, whose faces and
cultures stretch my heart sometimes to
breaking from sorrow and beauty,
sunrises and sunsets over water,
snow-covered mountains piercing the sky,
unimaginable poverty in Nairobi's shanty town,
polluted air belched from Gary Indiana
on the way east to DC and beyond

crumbling remains of ancient cities
marking human error and climate shifts,
diminishing bird populations and glaciers,
stark painted deserts and petroglyphs,
singing coyotes and lions wild in the night,
icebergs released into frigid waters

all etched upon my soul and recycled
into poetry and prose
to give back to the world
that calls me into being

— Elizabeth

taking risks

yesterday's boys
whooping with glee,
slide across the new ice
in their rubber boots,
while girls watch
from the edge of the pond,
their blue, cold hands
tucked in their armpits,
as the ice creaks and moans

today's girls
whooping with glee,
explore places once off-limit,
their shoes click across
shiny wood floors in
executive suites or
they don hiking boots
to traverse rugged mountain trails,
having learned by watching
to take risks

— Elizabeth

Sunday Women

Sunday women pull chairs
up to the table without haste.
They appear for breakfast,
pleasant, smiling, cordial.

Every strand of white hair
precisely in its place.
Earrings clipped on ears just-so.
Make-up meticulously applied
speaks discrete volumes
about years of practice.

Dressed in Sunday clothes
as though church-ready,
or perhaps prepared for
fashionable afternoon teas
or concerts at the end of the day.
But it is Monday, Tuesday —
                              not Sunday.

Do Sunday women
ever allow themselves
to be seen any other way?
Face-paint running from sweat
in the heat or wind-blown hair.

Do they appear at life's tragedies
dressed in Sunday-best,
no tears streaking cheeks when ·
told husbands or children are dead?

Or is their Sunday-best facade
a defensive shield against
indignities and ravages of old age,
         diminishment yet to come?

— Elizabeth

Road Kill

The event did not rate
    even a few lines in the media,
evidence two objects cannot
        occupy the same space.

Flashing lights, emergency vehicles
    two fire trucks, just in case,
police rerouted all traffic
    from the now impassable road,
a small red car stands at an angle,
        the motorcycle destroyed
beyond all recognition.

Splayed out on the pavement
        the man lies on his back,
    blood spreads out from his body,
his right arm jerks above his head
        as if it was searching
for the source of catastrophic damage
    while a standing figure sobs.

One hour later
    all signs of the event removed,
the bloody pavement flushed,
        cars stream in both directions,
    oblivious to one life stopped so suddenly.

                        — Elizabeth

Enough Time

Why are they laughing across the room?
Don't they know?

Don't they know the world is falling apart?
Humanity's future teeters for a foothold
on the head of a pin, having
pushed off all the angels.
Political games, financial collapse,
rebels trying to force out dictators,
children starving in numbers
too numerous to count.

They keep laughing.
Don't they know how much is at stake?
While inept leaders search for
solutions to unprecedented events.
When we have not had time to
catch our breath and grieve
what we have always known,
exchanged for some
brave new world not yet imagined.

They keep on laughing.
The warmth of their friendship
radiates across the room.

Perhaps they laugh
because there is enough time.
Time to love and hope.

— Elizabeth

Passages

When I was small, I was taught not to call attention to
myself. My mother imprinted her unspoken disapproval
upon me when I was five, for the mistake of winning
a radio contest by drawing what I could imagine while
        listening to Mussorgsky's *Night on Bald Mountain.*

Other friends relate similar stories. A teacher's disaproval
or classmates' ridicule so quickly dashes our satisfaction,
the message seared deep across our souls. So tender we
can be where coloring outside the lines, is a given, as we
venture forth with creative experiments and novel efforts.
        Quickly, we retreat inside and hide.

Until someday, the pain of what we have buried becomes
too great, and we fight our way beyond old wounds
        into the sunlight.

— Elizabeth

Gathered Lives

We are allotted only one life.
How then can we gather life together
into a whole piece that gives meaning?

Do we spread our arms wide open,
and scoop up life, to draw it
into the deepest recesses of our souls?

Or sit in quiet places and give back
to the universe the clutter of our days,
so we can hear what matters most?

Is the gathered life found
among crowds pushing up against
each other, desiring human connection?

Does it come from acknowledging
how little we know, then exploring our tithe
of wisdom in a multidimensional world?

Is it laughter and tears felt deeply
or learning to let go, so the new
can walk through the gates of our hearts?

Or is the only way to gather life
is by longing with every fiber of our being
for the questions and not the answers?

— Elizabeth

CHAPTER SIX

~ The Substance of Memories ~
Clem Nagel

Fleeting thoughts
reappear in dreams
for a while

~

Old red bricks fill holes
where open windows once were
gone, not forgotten

~

Forgiving comes hard
hold to your grudges gently
if dropped they might break

In Case They Return

As a young boy, I came across a large
heavy book about birds.
Who would have thought to put
a two-volume set
of T.S. Robert's classic *Birds of Minnesota*
in the school library
of our remote prairie town?

I must have been
the first to look inside.
The binding cracked a tell-tale sound.

The picture that appeared was
a Swallow-tailed Kite, a writhing snake
dangled from its talons.
I couldn't believe when I read that
kites were once numerous along
Winona's Mississippi River bluffs.

That's what I remember.

Years later, my mom and dad took me to
visit the Bell Natural History Museum.
There was one mounted so beautifully.
The background painting showed three kites
flying along river bluffs.
A pamphlet said that
they were no longer found in Minnesota.

That's what I remember.

Traveling in Costa Rica
with our grandson, we crossed
a windswept mountain summit, and in the near distance
we saw a hundred or so Swallow-tailed Kites
soaring gracefully down into a valley,
skimming over the forest canopy —
like butterflies.

That's what I remember.

I still keep my eyes open —
        in case they return

                                        — Clem

Grandpa's Flower

A blustery-cool,
    sun-warmed day in fall.
A crow-field with oaks.
A girl, near the start of her life,
    first sees them.
Crows — lined up
    within the mowed pattern on a
    gentle, grassy, oak hillside.

Why do they sit like that Grandpa?
    Beats me is my reply.
Crows join the wind as
    we pause at the stone bench
    by the circle's beginning.
Wind-blown oak leaves hide in the
    well-worn, sunken pathways.

Grandpa. What is this?
Carefully she steps into the labyrinth,
    begins to walk its path, cautiously.
But soon, she runs with abandon,
    pausing only to lie down and
    rest on the winding trail.
For a moment, oak leaves and
    long hair cover her face.

Then, up again, to walk and skip.
    The path leads her inward.
Ecstatic,
    she reaches the center
    with its six petals.
She sits down. Her eyes
    rest into the distance.

We saw Grandpa's flower,
    Grace tells her mother.

— Clem

—— *I recall an October afternoon, years earlier, when my granddaughter, then five years old, discovered a labyrinth mown in the grass. I did not tell her what it was, letting her discover it for herself.*

Marbles

My grandchildren have
fourteen computers of various sizes.
Some the size of a little notebook.

At their age, I had a lot of
marbles. More than fourteen!
All in a bag with
a drawstring.
Various sizes, shooters, steelies,
cat's eyes, all kinds.

Now, I worry about
losing my marbles.

— Clem

Interior Sounds

I

In the prairie, just north of town,
as young boy,
I walked along county roads.

An upland plover, landed on a
nearby fence post,
raised its wings
just before settling down.
Then came its haunting, flute-like,
ethereal whistle and
descending tremolo.

I listened
to the call from afar.
Never had I heard any bird
make such a sound.

Was another plover
listening?

II

Just north of town
a car sped along the highway.
From across a distant field,
I heard its sound

interrupting the prairie-quiet with
an ear piercing, whistling scream

as if the air objected to the way
the racing form intruded on
the early morning stillness.

Rhythmic, galloping, slapping
sound of smooth, worn tires on
unevenly poured concrete persists . . .
until the '57 Mercury disappeared.

Gone is the sound —
but not in my memory.
I wonder, does the prairie
scream back in return?

III

North of town, just west
of the Catholic Cemetery,
a springtime flock of
whistling swans rested

bedded down for the night on
black, freshly plowed dirt.

Their quiet calls
joined the evening stars.

Are they alone?

— Clem

— *I once traveled to Saskatchewan and heard that same ethereal call*
of the upland plover. I wonder if that spirit-sound is somewhere
within my soul?

A Tribute to My Science Teacher

I wish to thank you for keeping
all those drawers of labeled bird-skins.
They catapulted me into wanting
to see them in real life.

Thank you for those glass cabinets
full of ancient mouse specimens
swimming in formaldehyde,
so I could see them up-close without having to
kill them myself.

Thank you for telling our class
hummingbirds never land, because they
have no feet. I took my few friends
to watch the ruby-throats perch on wires
and nestle down in tiny nests.

You instilled in me a determination
to view life with eyes wide open.
For this I am grateful.

Sometimes, I wonder what
blind spots I harbor?

— Clem

CHAPTER SEVEN

~ Commentary on Daily Life ~
Elizabeth Nagel

He went to buy eggs
came home with blue hyacinths
perfume fills the house

~

Ordinary time
space between high points and feasts
just-baked bread and jam

~

On green freeway signs
pigeons perch above traffic
what are they thinking?

treasuring last times

yesterday we bought an apple tree
ready to burst into full-bloom
and stretch its roots out
when released from
the prison of its container

time together more precious
because it may be the last tree
we buy in our lives, a time to savor
because everything we do
may be for the last time

it is these everyday things
that carry the layers of our lives

— Elizabeth

Possibilities

What am I going to do today!
Life filled with possibilities.
Soak up the sacred.
Open my eyes wide.
Attend my breath.
Cultivate my curiosity.
Create open space for imagination.
Pull weeds, deadhead spent flowers.
Write.
Cook dinner.

It is truth I seek, not facts.

— Elizabeth

Looking for Spring

Groundhog-like, they crawl
out of their burrows and stretch their limbs
as they look around.
They smile in appreciation of neighbors
who chip ice loose around storm sewers,
to hasten the sun's movement
into a higher arc across the sky.

Running shoes donned, and sweatshirts,
along with gloves and hats
pulled down around ears,
for an early morning of jogging,
exhaled out-breath white before their faces.

Closets cleaned out with a vengeance,
muttering why they have kept
some things so long, now shoved into
boxes and sacks for Goodwill,
hoping others might have some use
for their no-longer needed discards.

Rakes rediscovered
in obscure corners of the garage,
they fill bags with the assorted debris
of the long winter and stack piles neatly
by the curb for garbage pick-up day.
Deck furniture hauled out of storage
along with memories of hot days
and backyard barbeques with friends.

Leaves gently pulled aside
in a search for snowdrops and
daffodils pushing through still icy soil,
they mark off days on the calendar
until the first pussy willows appear.

They rest a moment, leaning on rakes
and greet neighbors not seen
since last October or November.
Eying the grime on their cars,
they wonder if it might rain soon,
negating the need for one more
car wash visit.

Like groundhogs,
when the sun slips behind clouds and
the sky turns grey, their shadows disappear
they crawl back into their burrows,
grumbling and complaining,
suspicious they have been tricked,
that spring was only a mirage.

— Elizabeth

love poem

he gathers up armfuls
of garden debris,
last year's triumphs
now useless and brown

bending over, he gently
pulls away leaves covering
tender tulips, emerging promises
push away winter's sleep

the same gentle hands
as he held our new-born daughters,
marveling at the wonder of new life
just pushed from my womb

the same touch
I have felt when he cares
for me, when I am ill
life-protector, life-loving man

— Elizabeth

Important Snowpocalyptic Questions from the Effects of Being Snowbound

Do things fall out of people's pockets,
who live on the other side of the world?
After all, when I was a child
we believed that if you find a big hole
straight through and peer into it,
you would see the soles of their feet.

On the other side of the world
do birds fly upside down?
Or do they fly right-side up
peering into clouds for soft places
to lay eggs and raise their babes?

Instead of choosing blue,
are leaves on trees green,
because they want to match the grass?
If leaves were blue, it would mean
looking up through trees,
and not being able to tell blue sky
from thick crops of leaves.

Does snow fall sideways
in a blizzard because it surveys
the landscape, searching for
the best places to land?
And does ice hold tight to roads
so it won't slide away and become
lost in heaps of plowed snow?

If our brain did not invert what
our eyes actually see,
would we walk around believing
everything was upside down?
Feet in the air with our head
scraping along on the ground.
Like people who live
on the other side of the world,
with hands holding tight to pockets,
not wanting stuff to fall out.

— Elizabeth

lenten mind

my curmudgeonly mind would
rather grumble than be grateful
broken water softener, yesterday's
water bill evidence of its defection,
the car develops an ominous noise,
a bill buried on my desk
re-emerges two days late,
rejection notices fall from the mailbox,
why don't they like my poems?

perhaps I need to collect small grievances
in a pile in the middle of the room
and circle around it, chanting
harsh words to purge my system
of unwanted mineral deposits,
clean out closets and cupboards,
wash winter's film from windows

better yet, carry the mountain
of my grievances outside and torch it —
despite burning ordinances

— Elizabeth

no-speed zone

The road sign screams
pay attention
as I rush past
just over the speed limit.

Pay attention
as I absent-mindedly
remove chicken from
the freezer when hungry for fish.

The last rose nestled
among fat red hips
whispers *pay attention.*
I run down the list
of fall chores necessary
before snowfall.

My sweetheart touches
my shoulder when he walks past
and I am flooded
with joy and love.

Pay attention.

— Elizabeth

CHAPTER EIGHT

~ Soul Under Construction ~
Clem Nagel

*Water droplets dance
across the smooth water skin
melt into oneness*

~

*Music of wind chimes
pulsing calls of the lacewing
sounds of falling leaves*

~

*Gulls play with the wind
our boat slips down the Volga
banks of birch and pine*

Small Witness

We walk toward the
    early spring Carolina ocean —
        to be near the sea.

Fierce torrents of
    frigid rain and wind,
        blow slant against
            unprotected hands and faces.

A small girl stands
    in a pink hooded jacket,
        eyes resolute on the sea.

Her legs planted firmly in the sand,
    she leans into
        a wall of wind and water,
            raises her arms into the gale.

We witness her
    exhilaration and daring!

A signal of victorious conquest,
    maybe to no one but herself —
        or perhaps
            to the ocean.

                        — Clem

Questions for
Winter Oak Leaves

Brown leaves on silent trees,
why do you cling so tight?
Grasping twigs that
gave you birth?

Through winter's icy grip
and punishing winds,
you stay
you persevere.

> *Did I hear you say*
> *"we aren't done yet?"*
> *Are you holding*
> *your breath 'til spring?*

What will signal
winter's lessening?
Clinking of falling icicles,
like chiming
distant bells?

Come spring,
buds, surprised by warmth,
will swell beneath you.

Your dry leaves must
release and fall.
Announcing
to the warming earth

    let go, breathe,
    make way for the new,
    be aware of beauty
        in the present.

      —— Clem

—— *Winter is the season for paying closer attention to the commonplace.*
Notice how certain species of oak trees retain their leaves
throughout winter.

The Broken Toe

Settling down to write
at a café after lunch, the chatter
nearby is a comforting sound

    I overhear her
    say to a friend

Not quite certain
how it happened
Not anything amazing
or anything

It just broke

They say it will heal
all by itself
Not to worry

    In the meantime,
    I wonder —
    if old souls ever heal
    like that?

— Clem

Trust

Will there be anything left
when husks fall away?

Not much
but maybe enough.

Can water and air
penetrate the
shell
I allowed to
cover my soul?

I suspect my soul
needs to breathe
like trees
need to
breathe.

Who am I really?
Hoping for clarity,
trusting my
soul to survive.

— Clem

The Found

What is this?
    My hand
    touches something buried
    in the leaves and ground-cover.

My favorite garden pruners.
    The ones with red handles.
    I missed them for so long.
    Must have been two autumns ago.

Now found,
    with blades rusty, hinge frozen.
    Buried in mulch, close to
    the sweet autumn clematis vine.

I will
    clean, sharpen, polish, oil them.
    They will be
    as good as new.

Now, what about my life?

— Clem

Ring of Standing Stones: Orkney Islands

I pause,
touch each upright stone.
Press my ear to
lichen-etched surfaces.

> *Listen for*
> *the stone's heartbeats —*
> *at times deafening,*
> *pulsing*
> *through time.*

I am not the first
to touch
these ancient standing stones.
Nor the last.
They have been anchored
into this loved land
for millennia.

An Orkney Island farmer-guide,
tells how island families
live in respect —
at one with
their North Sea island landscape.

As stones, we have
secrets to keep.
Only sometimes do we
share our legends
with the clouds.

Were these stone sentinels harvested
nearby, or from somewhere
far distant?
How did ancient people move
these chiseled monoliths, leaving them
to face one another in
this circle by the sea?

We stones live as
a vulnerable presence
in your midst.
We sometimes bring
silent reminders
to the surface, and speak
of impermanence.

Did some stones fall
from the force of winter storms,
lightning strikes,
relentless freezing
and thawing of moisture
in crevices?

Listen to the inner
cracking of our souls.
Unheard by others
until a part of us leans
into hope
or falls away.

How long until a thin,
pleated slab separates
and comes to lie near its base?
When will new lichens
begin to grow?

Like mountains,
we become
worn down, forged
by water and ice
and endless winds.
By conversion of adversity
and hopelessness.

— Clem

— *I visited the ancient Ring of Brodgar, an early Bronze Age stone*
henge monument in the Ness of Brodgar on one of the Orkney
Islands, just north of Scotland. Of 60 original standing stones,
27 remain upright.

I have early childhood memories of listening to stones and even
imagining that I was one of them. I still put my ear to stones
and listen for what I might hear and feel.

I Am Thankful For

clear blue skies and
    spring fragrance of clove currant
        and lily of the valley

snow that melts
    for tulips pushing through
        thawing dirt

birds and butterflies
    resting in the
        afternoon sun

sounds of children's laughter
    and their parents
        joining in

the warm touch of
    my love's hand
        a glance from her brown eyes

people who live peace
    brave ones who
        dare follow them

remembering places
   where I have been and
      with whom
         I have journeyed

roads that lead nowhere
   and time to
      explore them

                    — Clem

Walking a Sand Beach in the Fog

The reality was, there were people
   all along the way
      but we walked the sand's edge
        together alone,
      because of the fog.

The sun was hidden,
   leaving nothing but gray and white
   and
   you and me.

Side by side,
   you barefoot, me in sandals
      like we always do.

Deep in my body, my heart
   turns and thinks of you.
      Deep in my heart, under the thick fog,
   the water moves back and forth.

Now, it's a slow walk,
   a peaceful walk like in sanctuary.
      We tire, decide to split up.
   I'll bring the car around,
     along the upper beach,
     to wherever you will be.

I walk back along the fog-shrouded way,
    alone, next to the water, where fog hangs
        where the sun should be.

I glance back to see you
    picking up precious shells,
        like you always do.

I look down at our foot prints, side by side, in the sand.
    Your bare feet and my sandals.
        I can tell every place you stopped for a shell,
    like you always do.

I glance back again.
    You are
        gone.
    Swallowed up in the fog.

A wave greets my feet and my
    footprints are now
        alone.

And I cry.

Later, we catch up
    with each other. I tell you
        I love you very much,
    like I always do.

                    — Clem

CHAPTER NINE

~ Cycles of Life ~
Elizabeth Nagel

Lead grey skies hold rain
lone red leaf floats on still pond
awaits winter snow

~

Children's voices drift
across the school soccer fields
on summer's last day

~

wild geese fly above
excited honking guides them
August practice runs

becoming sand

remains of winter snow melts
water seeps between layers
pieces crack loose
tumble down mountain sides
jagged edges not yet worn smooth
grey-tan layered upon purple
until small fragments
lie spent on cliff edges
waiting for summer rains to
shove them further down
into meadows and rivers
on the way seaward
to become warm sand beaches

new rock broken down over millennia
new faces exposed to light
for the first time
since their creation
when the earth was young

— Elizabeth

Turtle-life

early spring
turtles line the old tree
slanted out over the small pond
shorn of life, the grey trunk
polished over many winters

no space left vacant
from a distance the turtles
look like black scale insects
adhered to house-plants' stems

one quick motion
the startled turtles are gone
dark water settles again
in silence that conceals all

back down into the muck
to wait it out, this place of
return that preserves them during
the unforgiving freezing winter

then —
lure of sun-warmth
coaxes small turtle heads to break
the water's surface, they scramble
back onto the old tree
      to contemplate the day

          — Elizabeth

Earthquakes in Chile

The earth shudders.
A more superstitious generation
would say
the earth has had enough.

Tectonic plates
adjusting, shifting, rearranging.
Parallels to the evolution
of our human consciousness.

Is growth and change
ever easy?

— Elizabeth

a snail's life

over rock, its rasp tongue
gathers nourishment
until one day the snail
re-enters the universe's energy
leaving behind its house
a thing of beauty no longer needed

washed up by the sea
a small child finds
a snail shell half buried
in the sand, pockets it
while running her fingers
over its smoothness

the snail has entered
the cycle of life
in some other form
while its old house sits
on a shelf
in a child's room

— Elizabeth

embedded memories

she falls backward
into fresh snow
that creeps into her body warmth
waving her arms and legs
making snow angels
        laughing

she sprawls spread-eagled
in the meadow's heat
drinking in the blue sky
sweat running down her face
and into the rich earth
        laughing

she huddles in a hospital bed
blind eyes closed, remembering
cold snow, hot sun
meadow flowers, being loved
soon she will go home to the stars
        laughing

— Elizabeth

moving on

loyalty can be misplaced commitment
staying while I die inside by
hanging on to what was

a sign I fear the unknown more
until desperation drives me into
finally slamming doors behind me

without grace, when what I need
is a blessing ritual, then slip through
doorways, blow a kiss, and move on

— Elizabeth

transitions

discernment means looking back
choice points, roads taken believing
opportunities once passed are gone forever
only to find some circle back

discernment means looking forward
imagination, dreams woven into my soul
by the act of naming what might lie within
unbirthed, untried, denied

discernment means living in trust
knowing that after all my reflections
there is only the present to embrace
each moment a gift

— Elizabeth

clear mind, deep lakes

the sacred found me
first in mountain meadows
dense with summer growth
along stretched-out sand beaches
mist obscuring where horizon meets sky

the sacred called me
out of the tight confines
of childhood and invited me
to plunge into clear, cold northern lakes
mirroring the universe's midnight stars

now my aging body carries memories
of wild places I can no longer enter,
my world has shrunk,
while my soul has swollen
with wars, inequities, and destruction,
woven into the wild places I remember

I sit still, follow my breath
invite in the fractured world
breathe out healing compassion
the sacred still finds me
in the silence of deep lakes

— Elizabeth

ABOUT THE AUTHORS

Clem Nagel

Clem J. Nagel has lived in Minnesota most of his life, while traveling the world to pursue his love of the natural environment and the diversity of other cultures. Formally trained in theology, spiritual direction, and zoology, he has worked as a community organizer in a variety of efforts to improve services for others and to address social issues. Clem began writing poetry over a decade ago, when "poetry simply showed up" in his life. He loves teaching others to be attentive to the natural world and their own poetic voice. He believes writing poetry is a wonderful process for making discoveries about ourselves and the world in which we live.

Elizabeth Nagel

Elizabeth C. Nagel grew up on the prairie of western Minnesota. A few months after graduating from college, she left behind her childhood world of traditional role expectations for urban life of Washington DC during the sixties. Every professional work experience from physical biochemist to psychologist has brought Elizabeth to the place today where her primary passion is her work as a writer, poet, and fine arts photographer. With Clem, she has traveled the world and explored cultural expressions of other people's lives. She hopes her writing and photography may feed the souls of others in this conflicted and troubled world.